PRINCEWILL LAGANG

Blessed Unions: Christian Marriage Stories

First published by PRINCEWILL LAGANG 2023

Copyright © 2023 by Princewill Lagang

All rights reserved. No part of this publication may be reproduced, stored or transmitted in any form or by any means, electronic, mechanical, photocopying, recording, scanning, or otherwise without written permission from the publisher. It is illegal to copy this book, post it to a website, or distribute it by any other means without permission.

Princewill Lagang asserts the moral right to be identified as the author of this work.

First edition

*This book was professionally typeset on Reedsy.
Find out more at reedsy.com*

Contents

1	A Journey Begins	1
2	Love's Unwavering Promise	4
3	From Brokenness to Wholeness	7
4	Anchored in Hope	10
5	The Gift of Second Chances	12
6	When Faith Conquers Doubt	15
7	A Love Born of Service	18
8	Rekindling Lost Faith	21
9	Finding Love in Unexpected Places	24
10	A Love Restored	27
11	A Legacy of Love	30
12	A Love That Endures	33

1

A Journey Begins

Title: "Blessed Unions: Christian Marriage Stories"

In a small, picturesque town nestled in the heart of the Appalachian Mountains, the sun's first rays gently kissed the sleepy landscape. The town was named Harmonyville, and it was a place where tranquility and spirituality seemed to coexist harmoniously, much like the couples whose stories we will soon delve into.

Blessed Unions: Christian Marriage Stories is a collection of tales that illustrate the extraordinary, often heartwarming, and sometimes challenging journeys of couples united by their faith in God and love for one another. These are stories of ordinary people experiencing the extraordinary; tales that celebrate the sanctity of marriage through the lens of Christian devotion.

The curtain rises on this captivating anthology with the story of Ethan and Sarah, a young couple whose love story epitomized the ideals of faith, hope, and love. Their story is the embodiment of Ephesians 5:31, which proclaims, "For this reason, a man shall leave his father and mother and be joined to his wife, and the two shall become one flesh."

BLESSED UNIONS: CHRISTIAN MARRIAGE STORIES

Chapter 1: A Journey Begins

Ethan gazed out of the window of their cozy, rustic cabin. The morning fog hung in the air, giving the mountain scenery an ethereal quality. He was a sturdy, God-fearing man, with a heart as big as the hills that surrounded their home. As the sun pierced through the mist, he couldn't help but smile. He thanked the Lord for the day and, more importantly, for Sarah.

Sarah, his beloved, was busy in the kitchen. The aroma of fresh-baked bread filled the cabin. She had a natural grace and a laugh that could melt the heart of even the sternest preacher. The couple was preparing for a gathering later that day, celebrating their first wedding anniversary. As they hustled and bustled in the kitchen, Ethan couldn't help but reflect on the journey that had brought them here.

It all began five years ago when they first met in the Harmonyville Community Church. Both were deeply rooted in their faith, and their love for Jesus drew them closer together from the start. Their courtship was a testament to the patience and commitment required in a godly relationship. They had spent many evenings sitting on the porch of Sarah's childhood home, talking about their dreams, their faith, and the future they hoped to build together.

Their union was not without its challenges. The journey to their wedding day was filled with trials that tested their love and faith. Sarah's father's sudden illness had cast a shadow of uncertainty over their plans, but their unwavering belief in the power of prayer, and the love they had for each other, saw them through the darkest of times. Their wedding day was a testament to the support and love of their church community, who rallied around them to make the day truly special.

As they sat down to break bread together, Ethan and Sarah offered a prayer of gratitude to the Lord for bringing them together and for guiding them through the trials and tribulations of life. Their faith had not only sustained them but had also deepened their love.

Blessed Unions: Christian Marriage Stories explores the rich tapestry of Christian love stories, like Ethan and Sarah's, which serve as a testament to the power of faith, love, and the enduring bonds of holy matrimony. Each chapter in this anthology will uncover new narratives of devotion, trials, and triumphs that inspire and uplift, proving that love, when rooted in faith, can conquer all.

In the following chapters, we'll explore more remarkable tales of Christian couples who have embarked on their sacred journeys in faith. Each story is a unique thread in the tapestry of God's divine plan, a celebration of the blessed unions that fill our lives with hope, love, and the enduring power of faith.

2

Love's Unwavering Promise

Title: "Blessed Unions: Christian Marriage Stories"

As the sun painted the sky with shades of coral and lavender, a different love story begins to unfurl in the pages of our anthology, "Blessed Unions: Christian Marriage Stories." This time, we venture into the heart of the bustling city of Riverdale, where love and faith converge in the lives of Mark and Emily, two souls bound together by God's hand.

Chapter 2: Love's Unwavering Promise

Riverdale, a city of endless possibilities and constant motion, served as the backdrop for Mark and Emily's remarkable love story. Mark was a driven entrepreneur, deeply committed to his faith, and Emily was a compassionate nurse with a heart full of kindness and a soul ablaze with devotion. Their paths first crossed in the bustling corridors of Riverdale General Hospital.

Mark was visiting a close friend who was receiving treatment. As he sat in the hospital chapel, he noticed Emily, her soft voice carrying the melodies of a hymn through the chapel's open door. Something about her presence, her genuine faith, and her ethereal voice struck a chord within him. Mark felt an irresistible pull to get to know her better.

Their courtship was a delicate dance, each step guided by faith. Mark found himself attending church events more frequently, striking up conversations with Emily after Sunday service, and offering his support to her as she cared for her patients. Emily, in turn, was moved by Mark's unwavering commitment to God, which reflected in his daily life and his business practices. It was clear to her that he was a man of faith and integrity.

Their love story was not without challenges. Mark's demanding career often led to late nights at the office, causing them to spend less time together. Emily's nursing job was no less demanding, with long shifts that sometimes stretched into the early hours of the morning. In these trials, their faith served as an anchor. They prayed together, seeking God's guidance and strength to navigate the stormy seas of their careers and commitments.

After years of courting, Mark decided to pop the question. Underneath a canopy of twinkling stars and the soft glow of city lights, he proposed to Emily in the hospital's rooftop garden. Surrounded by their friends and the comforting presence of God, Emily tearfully accepted, and they began planning their wedding.

Their wedding day was a testament to their faith and the unwavering promise they had made to each other and to God. In the presence of their families, friends, and the Riverdale church community, Mark and Emily exchanged vows and committed their lives to one another. The love that had blossomed between them was a testament to the beauty of a union rooted in faith, and the chapter of their marriage had only just begun.

"Love's Unwavering Promise" is a story that explores the trials and triumphs of two people who found love in the midst of life's bustling chaos, bound together by their shared faith in God. Their journey reminds us that love, when intertwined with faith, can endure the trials of the world and shine ever more brightly, like a beacon of hope in the darkest night.

The following chapters of "Blessed Unions: Christian Marriage Stories" will continue to unveil inspiring love stories, each unique in its challenges and triumphs but sharing a common foundation of faith in Christ and the enduring power of love.

3

From Brokenness to Wholeness

Title: "Blessed Unions: Christian Marriage Stories"

In our anthology, "Blessed Unions: Christian Marriage Stories," we now turn our attention to a love story that beautifully illustrates the transformative power of faith and love. Join us as we journey through the captivating narrative of Michael and Sarah, a couple whose union served as a testament to the healing grace of God.

Chapter 3: From Brokenness to Wholeness

In the bustling city of Greenwood, amidst the hustle and bustle of life, Michael and Sarah's paths collided. Yet, it wasn't a chance encounter; it was a divine orchestration. Both Michael and Sarah had experienced their share of life's hardships, and it was their faith that eventually brought them together.

Michael, a talented musician and songwriter, had lived a life marked by the ebb and flow of addiction. His journey was tumultuous, filled with trials and relapses, but he never lost sight of his faith. Sarah, on the other hand, was a therapist who had dedicated her life to helping others overcome their struggles, even though she carried her own scars of a painful past.

Their paths crossed at a church support group for individuals battling addiction. Michael, seeking spiritual guidance and support on his path to recovery, attended the group meetings, where he first noticed Sarah. Her unwavering faith and dedication to helping others struck a chord within him. Her gentle encouragement, coupled with the grace of God, slowly began to heal the brokenness in his life.

Sarah, too, saw something special in Michael. His deep love for God, his undeniable talent, and his willingness to confront his demons resonated with her own journey towards healing. She knew they shared a connection rooted in their faith, and as their friendship deepened, they found themselves leaning on each other for support and guidance.

Love grew between them, a love that was tempered by adversity and strengthened through their shared faith. They prayed together, and their shared devotion helped them navigate the turbulent waters of recovery and healing. The power of God's love became the cornerstone of their relationship, transforming their brokenness into wholeness.

When Michael proposed to Sarah, it was more than a declaration of love; it was a testament to the healing and transformation they had experienced together. In a church filled with friends and family who had witnessed their individual journeys to redemption, they exchanged vows, promising to walk the path of faith and recovery together, trusting that God's grace would guide their way.

From brokenness to wholeness, their love story is a powerful reminder that faith can heal even the deepest of wounds. Michael and Sarah's journey demonstrates that God's love can bring redemption and restoration to the lives of those who seek Him, and that love, when rooted in faith, can triumph over adversity.

Chapter 3, "From Brokenness to Wholeness," is a poignant tale of redemption and transformation, highlighting the profound impact of faith and love on two individuals who emerged from their struggles as a testament to God's grace.

As we continue to explore the pages of "Blessed Unions: Christian Marriage Stories," we'll encounter more inspiring narratives of couples whose love stories are woven with threads of faith, grace, and love, reflecting the beauty of God's plan for their lives.

4

Anchored in Hope

Title: "Blessed Unions: Christian Marriage Stories"

In the pages of our anthology, "Blessed Unions: Christian Marriage Stories," we turn our attention to a story of resilience, hope, and the enduring strength of faith. Join us as we dive into the narrative of David and Rebecca, a couple whose love weathered the storm and emerged anchored in the hope found in God.

Chapter 4: Anchored in Hope

Their journey began in the coastal town of Seaview, a place where the sea's tumultuous waves mirrored the challenges David and Rebecca would face. David was a dedicated fisherman, a man of strong character, deeply rooted in his faith. Rebecca, a schoolteacher, had a heart full of compassion and a spirit unyielding to life's hardships. Their paths crossed in the most unexpected way when a violent storm struck Seaview, wreaking havoc on the town.

As the town grappled with the aftermath of the storm, David, along with the other fishermen, had to rebuild their livelihoods from the ground up. The task was daunting, and the future seemed uncertain. It was during this time that David and Rebecca, who had volunteered to help with the relief efforts, met. David was struck by her kindness and unwavering commitment to her students, even in the face of adversity. Rebecca admired his resilience and his unshakable trust in God's plan.

Their love story was an ode to hope. As they worked side by side to restore Seaview, they found solace in each other's company. They prayed together, seeking God's guidance in the tumultuous sea of life, and their shared faith was the anchor that kept them grounded in the most trying of times.

David and Rebecca's love deepened, even as they faced numerous challenges in their relationship. The trials of their respective jobs often kept them apart, and the scars of the storm continued to affect the community. Yet, their unwavering faith in God's providence and their love for one another sustained them.

When David proposed to Rebecca, it was on a windswept beach, where the waves roared in the distance, a constant reminder of the trials they had overcome together. Their wedding, held in the local church filled with friends and neighbors, was a testament to the enduring power of hope and faith. In their vows, they declared their commitment to stand by each other, regardless of the storms life might bring.

"Anchored in Hope" is a story that illuminates the beauty of love that persists in the face of adversity. David and Rebecca's journey is a reminder that, through faith and hope, couples can weather any storm and emerge even stronger, like a ship anchored securely in the harbor.

As we continue to explore the stories within "Blessed Unions: Christian Marriage Stories," we will encounter more narratives of hope, faith, and love, each unique in its challenges and triumphs but united by the thread of Christian devotion that weaves through them.

5

The Gift of Second Chances

Title: "Blessed Unions: Christian Marriage Stories"

Within the pages of our anthology, "Blessed Unions: Christian Marriage Stories," we delve into a narrative that demonstrates the profound power of redemption and second chances. Join us in the story of John and Laura, a couple whose love story is a testimony to the transformative grace of God.

Chapter 5: The Gift of Second Chances

Their journey began in the heart of the city of New Hope. John, a successful lawyer, and Laura, a dedicated pediatric nurse, were both familiar with the fast-paced life and the demands it placed on their souls. Yet, their paths had been marked by separate trials, and it was only when they met that they began to grasp the true meaning of redemption.

John had lived a life of privilege and success, but his ambition had led him down a dark path, causing him to neglect the very values and faith he had been raised with. It was only after a personal crisis, brought about by a near-fatal car accident, that he began to reevaluate his life. John found solace in a small church that had been visited by his parents for years, a place where he rekindled his relationship with God and his faith.

Laura, on the other hand, had faced her share of personal tragedies. A painful divorce had left her emotionally scarred, and it seemed as though love had abandoned her. But her devotion to her young patients and her strong faith provided the strength she needed to keep moving forward.

Their paths converged at John's home church. There, during a Sunday service, they met and struck up a conversation. Laura's compassionate nature and her deep faith instantly resonated with John, and he found in her a guiding light back to his faith and values. Laura, in turn, was drawn to John's dedication to his newfound spiritual journey.

Their relationship grew slowly, built on a foundation of trust and shared faith. They both recognized the power of second chances and redemption, which their faith provided. They prayed together, asking for guidance and forgiveness, and their love blossomed amidst the backdrop of the church that had brought them together.

When John proposed to Laura, it was in the same church that had played such a pivotal role in their journey. Surrounded by the support of their families and the church community, they exchanged vows. Their wedding was a testament to the gift of second chances, redemption, and the transformative power of God's grace.

"The Gift of Second Chances" is a story that illuminates the beauty of love born from redemption. John and Laura's journey is a reminder that, through faith and the embrace of God's grace, couples can find love and hope even after they've weathered life's most challenging storms.

As we continue to explore the stories within "Blessed Unions: Christian Marriage Stories," we will encounter more narratives of redemption, faith, and love, each unique in its challenges and triumphs but united by the thread of Christian devotion that weaves through them.

6

When Faith Conquers Doubt

Title: "Blessed Unions: Christian Marriage Stories"

In our anthology, "Blessed Unions: Christian Marriage Stories," we now venture into a love story that explores the profound journey from doubt to faith. Join us as we delve into the narrative of James and Grace, a couple whose union embodies the transformative power of unwavering faith.

Chapter 6: When Faith Conquers Doubt

The story of James and Grace unfolds in the tranquil town of Havenbrook. Both had grown up in devout Christian families, but their paths to love and marriage were laden with doubt, which ultimately gave way to unshakable faith.

James, a scholar and theologian, had spent years exploring the intricate depths of religious philosophy. His quest for knowledge led him to question and, at times, doubt the very faith that had defined his upbringing. Grace, on the other hand, was a nurse with a heart that brimmed with compassion. She had weathered a series of personal trials that had left her with lingering doubts about the goodness of God.

Their paths crossed at a theological conference in Havenbrook, where James was presenting a paper on his theological doubts, and Grace was attending as a volunteer nurse. Despite their different paths, they were drawn to each other's inner conflicts. James saw in Grace a nurturing spirit that was different from the rigid theology he had been accustomed to, while Grace was intrigued by James's intellectual curiosity and his willingness to confront doubt.

Their initial interactions were marked by debates and discussions on matters of faith, belief, and the existence of God. Grace shared her experiences as a nurse, caring for the sick and the suffering, which had led her to question God's purpose. James, in turn, shared his scholarly insights and the questions that had haunted him for years.

What emerged from their spirited conversations was a bond, built on mutual respect and a shared journey from doubt to faith. They began to pray together, seeking answers from a higher power, and their connection deepened as they found solace in their shared pursuit of spiritual understanding.

Their courtship, marked by a dance between doubt and faith, led them to the realization that doubt need not be a stumbling block but a stepping stone to deeper faith. When James proposed to Grace, it was under the canopy of a starlit night in Havenbrook, where they had first met. Surrounded by their loved ones, they exchanged vows in a ceremony that celebrated their journey of questioning and discovery, ultimately leading to a profound and unshakable faith.

"When Faith Conquers Doubt" is a story that highlights the transformative power of faith and the beauty of finding love amidst the complexities of doubt. James and Grace's journey reminds us that faith can emerge from the most unlikely of places and that love, rooted in unwavering faith, can conquer even the deepest of doubts.

As we continue to explore the stories within "Blessed Unions: Christian Marriage Stories," we will encounter more narratives of faith, doubt, and love, each unique in its challenges and triumphs but united by the thread of Christian devotion that weaves through them.

7

A Love Born of Service

Title: "Blessed Unions: Christian Marriage Stories"

In our anthology, "Blessed Unions: Christian Marriage Stories," we now journey into a love story that reflects the beauty of a shared commitment to service and faith. Join us as we delve into the narrative of Samuel and Rebecca, a couple whose union is a testament to love, selflessness, and devotion to their Christian beliefs.

Chapter 7: A Love Born of Service

Their story unfolds in the bustling city of Gracefield, where Samuel and Rebecca each pursued careers dedicated to serving their community. Samuel, a firefighter, and Rebecca, a social worker, shared a common desire to make the world a better place, and their faith in Christ was the guiding force behind their selfless pursuits.

Samuel was known for his courage and dedication in the face of danger. He had always been a person of faith, finding solace and strength in his relationship with God during his challenging job. Rebecca, in her role as a social worker, was deeply compassionate, extending her care to the most vulnerable members of society.

Their paths converged during a community event organized by the local church. It was there that Samuel, a volunteer firefighter at the event, met Rebecca, who was coordinating services for the needy. As they worked side by side, they recognized the common thread of compassion and faith that bound them together.

Their love story unfolded as they continued their work, side by side, in the service of others. Together, they found a deep connection not only in their shared faith but also in their shared commitment to improving the lives of those they encountered. They prayed together, not only for their own relationship but for the well-being of the people they served.

As their love deepened, so did their understanding of the significance of faith in their lives. They realized that their faith was not just a personal connection with God but a shared source of strength that sustained their love and service to others. This understanding was the cornerstone of their relationship.

When Samuel proposed to Rebecca, he did so during a charity event they had organized together. Surrounded by volunteers and the people they had served, he asked her to be his partner in life, a partner in faith and in service. Their wedding, held in the church where they had first met, was a celebration of their love, their devotion to God, and their shared commitment to making the world a better place.

"A Love Born of Service" is a story that underscores the profound power of love rooted in selflessness and faith. Samuel and Rebecca's journey is a testament to the transformative nature of love that emerges from a shared commitment to service and a shared faith in Christ.

As we continue to explore the stories within "Blessed Unions: Christian Marriage Stories," we will encounter more narratives of love, service, and faith, each unique in its challenges and triumphs but united by the thread of Christian devotion that weaves through them.

8

Rekindling Lost Faith

Title: "Blessed Unions: Christian Marriage Stories"

In our anthology, "Blessed Unions: Christian Marriage Stories," we delve into a poignant love story that explores the journey of rediscovering faith and love. Join us as we explore the narrative of Matthew and Sarah, a couple whose union is marked by the rekindling of their faith in God and in each other.

Chapter 8: Rekindling Lost Faith

Matthew and Sarah's journey begins in the picturesque town of Willowbrook. Their story is one of love lost and found, and the transformative power of faith to mend what was once broken.

In their youth, Matthew and Sarah were childhood sweethearts, deeply devoted to each other and their faith. Their shared love for God was the cornerstone of their relationship. They dreamed of a future together, full of hope and shared devotion.

However, life had a way of intervening in their plans. Matthew's family had to relocate to another city, and the young couple was separated. The distance, combined with the challenges of early adulthood, led them to drift apart. As they pursued their individual paths, they also began to lose touch with their faith.

Years passed, and both experienced their share of trials and tribulations. Matthew's career in finance left him feeling unfulfilled, while Sarah, a teacher, had faced personal hardships that had shaken her belief in the goodness of life and the presence of God. They had both lost their way and, in the process, each other.

Their paths converged unexpectedly when they returned to Willowbrook for a high school reunion. As they exchanged stories and rekindled old memories, a spark of their former connection ignited. The nostalgia of their shared faith and love for God began to resurface, and they found themselves drawn back to each other.

The reunion awakened within them a longing to rekindle their faith, not just individually but also as a couple. They began to attend church together, seeking guidance and solace in their renewed relationship with God. The strength of their rekindled faith also breathed new life into their love for each other.

As their love blossomed anew, Matthew proposed to Sarah during a visit to the same church they had attended as children. Surrounded by friends and family, they pledged their love and commitment to each other and to their shared faith. Their wedding was a celebration of the redemption and restoration that had occurred in their lives and their relationship.

"Rekindling Lost Faith" is a story that celebrates the power of love and faith to heal, restore, and rekindle what was once lost. Matthew and Sarah's journey is a reminder that, even in moments of doubt and separation, faith can be reignited, and love can be rediscovered.

As we continue to explore the stories within "Blessed Unions: Christian Marriage Stories," we will encounter more narratives of lost and found love, faith, and the transformative power of God's grace, each unique in its challenges and triumphs but united by the thread of Christian devotion that weaves through them.

9

Finding Love in Unexpected Places

Title: "Blessed Unions: Christian Marriage Stories"

In our anthology, "Blessed Unions: Christian Marriage Stories," we journey into a narrative of serendipity and divine intervention. Join us as we delve into the story of Mark and Rachel, a couple whose love story unfolded in the most unexpected of places.

Chapter 9: Finding Love in Unexpected Places

Mark and Rachel's story takes place in the vibrant city of Providence, where the bustling streets and thriving businesses belie the quiet and profound love story that would emerge.

Mark, a skilled architect, had dedicated his life to creating spaces of beauty and functionality. Despite his artistic talents, he had been unable to find a lasting connection in his personal life. Rachel, a librarian with a passion for literature and a deep love for the church, had faced her share of heartbreak as well. Their paths crossed when Mark was assigned to work on a project to design a new library for the city.

From the moment they met, Mark and Rachel felt an inexplicable connection. There was an unspoken understanding between them, a sense that they were kindred spirits. As Mark began to discuss the project with Rachel and the library committee, their professional interactions deepened into a meaningful friendship.

Rachel's faith and love for the church played a significant role in her life, and Mark was profoundly touched by her devotion. As he attended the church services with her, he found himself drawn to the sermons, the hymns, and the sense of community. Rachel, in turn, was captivated by Mark's creativity and his ability to bring beauty to the world through his architectural designs.

Their shared experiences led to heartfelt conversations about faith, values, and the desires of their hearts. Both had experienced the trials of life, but they found solace and hope in each other's presence. Their friendship evolved into a profound love rooted in their shared faith and an understanding of the importance of spiritual connection in a relationship.

When Mark proposed to Rachel, he did so in the library he had designed for the city, a place that had brought them together in the first place. Surrounded by the scent of freshly printed books and the grandeur of the space, he asked her to be his partner for life. Their wedding, held in the city's historic church, was a testament to the love that had blossomed between them in the most unexpected of places.

"Finding Love in Unexpected Places" is a story that celebrates the serendipity of love and the way God works in mysterious ways to bring two souls together. Mark and Rachel's journey reminds us that love can find us in the most unexpected places, and that faith, when shared, can deepen the bond between two people.

As we continue to explore the stories within "Blessed Unions: Christian Marriage Stories," we will encounter more narratives of love, faith, and divine intervention, each unique in its challenges and triumphs but united by the thread of Christian devotion that weaves through them.

10

A Love Restored

Title: "Blessed Unions: Christian Marriage Stories"

In the final chapter of our anthology, "Blessed Unions: Christian Marriage Stories," we delve into a love story that exemplifies the resilience of the human spirit and the enduring power of faith. Join us as we explore the narrative of Daniel and Maria, a couple whose union is a testament to the restoration of love and the transformative grace of God.

Chapter 10: A Love Restored

Daniel and Maria's story unfolds in the quaint town of Rivertown, a place where the scenic riverbanks and cozy homes concealed the pain and redemption of their love story. Their journey is one marked by the dissolution of their marriage, the subsequent rediscovery of their faith, and the miraculous restoration of their love.

In the early years of their marriage, Daniel and Maria had been deeply in love, their shared faith a cornerstone of their relationship. They had built a life together, filled with dreams and aspirations. However, life's challenges, miscommunications, and the strains of everyday existence began to erode the foundation of their love.

Their marriage began to unravel, and they found themselves growing distant, struggling to communicate, and losing the deep connection that had once defined their love. Eventually, they made the painful decision to separate, their hearts heavy with regret and sorrow.

During their time apart, Daniel and Maria independently embarked on spiritual journeys, seeking solace and healing. They each found refuge in their faith, attending separate churches and engaging in spiritual practices to cope with the pain of their separation. Their shared faith was, ironically, the very thing that had led them to question and ultimately strengthen their own spiritual lives.

Years passed, and their separate paths brought them back to Rivertown. As fate would have it, they encountered each other during a local charity event organized by their respective churches. The encounter was marked by a mixture of emotions—surprise, regret, and a flicker of hope.

Their reconnection was awkward and tentative at first, but as they engaged in heartfelt conversations, they recognized the profound spiritual growth that had occurred in their lives during their separation. They shared their individual experiences of restoration, forgiveness, and the power of faith to heal. It was clear that their journey back to God had also led them back to each other.

Their love rekindled, stronger and more profound than ever. They realized that, through faith and the transformative grace of God, their marriage could be restored. They prayed together, seeking God's guidance and forgiveness for the past, and in the process, they discovered that their faith could mend the wounds of their relationship.

When Daniel proposed to Maria, he did so in the very church where they had originally exchanged vows. Surrounded by the supportive embrace of their renewed faith and their church community, they pledged their love and commitment to each other once more. Their wedding was a celebration of a love that had been tested and restored through the power of faith and divine intervention.

"A Love Restored" is a story that celebrates the resilience of love and the transformative grace of God in restoring what was once broken. Daniel and Maria's journey reminds us that even the most fractured relationships can be healed, rekindled, and renewed through faith and the redemptive power of love.

As we conclude our exploration of "Blessed Unions: Christian Marriage Stories," we have encountered a tapestry of narratives that celebrate the beauty of love, faith, and devotion. Each story is unique, reflecting the challenges and triumphs of Christian couples, united by the thread of faith that weaves through their lives and love stories.

11

A Legacy of Love

Title: "Blessed Unions: Christian Marriage Stories"

In this bonus chapter of our anthology, "Blessed Unions: Christian Marriage Stories," we celebrate a couple whose enduring love and unwavering faith have left an indelible mark not only on their own lives but on the lives of those around them. Join us as we explore the heartwarming narrative of Samuel and Elizabeth, a couple whose union embodies the idea of leaving a legacy of love.

Chapter 11: A Legacy of Love

Samuel and Elizabeth's love story takes place in the picturesque town of Harmonyville, a place where generations of families have built their lives around faith and community. Samuel, a retired pastor, and Elizabeth, a devoted volunteer in the church, had spent a lifetime cultivating their love and faith in a way that continues to inspire and uplift others.

Their journey together began in their youth, as they attended the same church and grew up within a close-knit community of faith. They shared common values and dreams, centered on their deep love for God and the desire to serve others. After a courtship rooted in faith, they married and embarked on a life of ministry.

Samuel's career as a pastor and Elizabeth's dedication to church activities made them beloved figures in their community. They offered spiritual guidance, comfort, and support to countless individuals and families over the years. Their marriage served as an example of love, devotion, and faith that inspired those around them.

Through their shared commitment to the church and its members, Samuel and Elizabeth not only built a strong and loving family but also touched the lives of countless others. Their kindness, wisdom, and faith left an enduring mark on those they met.

Their legacy of love extended to their children, who were raised with the same values and commitment to faith. Today, their family continues to serve the church and the community, carrying forward the tradition of love and devotion that Samuel and Elizabeth had established.

As Samuel and Elizabeth approach their golden years, they find themselves surrounded by the warmth and appreciation of those whose lives they've touched. They continue to be a source of inspiration, serving as a living testament to the enduring power of love rooted in faith.

"A Legacy of Love" is a story that celebrates a love that endures and serves as an example for generations to come. Samuel and Elizabeth's journey reminds us that a love founded in faith can create a legacy of inspiration and service, shaping not only their own lives but the lives of those they've touched.

As we conclude our journey through the pages of "Blessed Unions: Christian Marriage Stories," we've encountered a tapestry of narratives that celebrate the beauty of love, faith, and devotion. Each story is unique, reflecting the challenges and triumphs of Christian couples, united by the thread of faith that weaves through their lives and love stories, leaving a legacy of love that inspires and uplifts.

12

A Love That Endures

Title: "Blessed Unions: Christian Marriage Stories"

In this final chapter of our anthology, "Blessed Unions: Christian Marriage Stories," we explore a love story that stands the test of time, demonstrating the enduring power of faith and devotion. Join us as we delve into the narrative of Peter and Susan, a couple whose union is a shining example of love's endurance.

Chapter 12: A Love That Endures

Peter and Susan's story unfolds in the quiet village of Evergreen, a place where time seems to slow, allowing their love to deepen and flourish over the years. Their journey is one marked by decades of shared faith, unwavering commitment, and the enduring love that has stood the test of time.

The couple first crossed paths during their teenage years in Evergreen. They were drawn together by their mutual involvement in church activities and shared values rooted in their Christian faith. It wasn't long before they realized that their bond ran deeper than friendship.

After a courtship filled with walks through the village and evenings spent stargazing, Peter and Susan married in a simple ceremony in the village's historic church. Their love story had only just begun, and they were eager to face life's adventures together.

Over the years, Peter and Susan encountered their share of challenges, both as individuals and as a couple. The trials of parenthood, the demands of work, and the inevitable obstacles of life tried to test the strength of their love. But their shared faith served as an anchor that kept their marriage steady, even during the most turbulent of times.

Their devotion to God and each other was a constant source of strength. They found solace in attending church services together, often holding hands as they sang hymns and listened to sermons that nourished their souls. Their shared faith was not just a part of their lives; it was the very essence of their love.

As Peter and Susan entered their golden years, their love had matured into a deep, enduring bond. They'd seen the world together, celebrated milestones together, and weathered storms together. Their love had transformed from youthful passion into a profound companionship, rooted in the faith that had sustained them.

When Peter proposed to Susan again on their fiftieth wedding anniversary, it was a simple, heartfelt gesture. Surrounded by their children and grandchildren, they renewed their vows in the same church where they had married. Their love had come full circle, a testament to the enduring power of faith and devotion.

"A Love That Endures" is a story that celebrates the beauty of a love that stands the test of time. Peter and Susan's journey reminds us that love, when rooted in faith and unwavering commitment, can flourish and endure, remaining a constant source of strength and joy, even as the years pass.

As we conclude our exploration of "Blessed Unions: Christian Marriage Stories," we've encountered a tapestry of narratives that celebrate the beauty of love, faith, and devotion. Each story is unique, reflecting the challenges and triumphs of Christian couples, united by the thread of faith that weaves through their lives and love stories.

Book Summary: "Blessed Unions: Christian Marriage Stories"

"Blessed Unions: Christian Marriage Stories" is an inspiring anthology that offers readers a captivating glimpse into the profound love stories of Christian couples. Within its pages, this anthology reveals the beauty of love, faith, and devotion that weaves through the lives of these couples, each facing their unique trials and triumphs.

Spanning twelve chapters, the book explores diverse love stories, each illuminating the transformative power of faith. From tales of redemption to stories of serendipity, the narratives within this anthology showcase the ways in which love can be rekindled, restored, and even passed down through generations.

The stories unfold in a variety of settings, from bustling cities to tranquil towns, and they introduce us to couples with diverse backgrounds and challenges. We meet couples who met through shared missions of service, those who journeyed from doubt to faith, and others who found love in the most unexpected places.

Each chapter presents a new couple and their unique journey. We witness the healing power of faith as it mends brokenness, confronts doubt, and rekindles love. The stories emphasize the transformative grace of God, demonstrating that love, when rooted in faith, can overcome adversity, trials, and even the passage of time.

As we journey through the anthology, we encounter not only the trials and triumphs of love but also the profound role of faith in these couples' lives. Each story serves as a reminder that faith can be a guiding force, a source of strength, and a means of redemption. It shows that love, when intertwined with devotion, can create enduring unions that leave a legacy of inspiration and service.

In the final chapters, we meet couples whose love stories have stood the test of time, celebrating their enduring love and unwavering faith. These narratives reveal that love, when deeply rooted in faith, can withstand the trials of life and grow into a profound companionship that endures for a lifetime.

"Blessed Unions: Christian Marriage Stories" is a celebration of love, faith, and devotion that inspires and uplifts. The anthology serves as a testament to the enduring power of love, the transformative grace of God, and the beauty of Christian devotion in the context of marriage. It is a heartwarming collection that showcases the resilience of love and the enduring legacy of faith in the lives of these remarkable couples.

www.ingramcontent.com/pod-product-compliance
Lightning Source LLC
LaVergne TN
LVHW010440070526
838199LV00066B/6106